My Own Reconciliation Booklet

Name

My first celebration of the Sacrament of Reconciliation:

Date

Parish

City

State

I Am God's Friend

I know that I'm special to God. I'm his friend.

Sometimes I make a choice that doesn't show love for God or others. This hurts my friendship with him. I sin.

When I sin, I can say this to let God know that I'm sorry.

_____

_____

_____

_____

_____

_____

_____

God forgives me in the Sacrament of Reconciliation.

Draw your happy face in the frame.

This is my happy face after I say "I'm sorry."

I Prepare for the Sacrament of Reconciliation

I can celebrate the Sacrament of Reconciliation in two ways: with the community or individually.

I can confess my sins to the priest in two ways: face-to-face or from behind a screen.

But first I pray to the Holy Spirit for help.
I can pray with these words.

You can color these words.

Holy Spirit,

you show me how to love. Help me know

love.

when I have failed to **love.** *Help me*

confess

my sins and ask for

forgiveness.

Amen.

Or I can use my own words.

Holy Spirit, _____

_____

_____

_____

_____

_____

I Make an Examination of Conscience

I review the Ten Commandments. I ask myself questions like these.

My Relationship with God

Do I pray to God each day?

Do I pay attention and do my part at Mass?

Do I use God's name or Jesus' name when I am angry?

My Relationship with Others

Do I obey my parents and teachers?

Do I follow the rules at school and at home?

Do I treat others fairly?

Do I make fun of others?

Do I fight at home or on the playground?

Do I take care of my belongings and those of others?

I name to myself the sins I need to confess. Now I am ready to celebrate the Sacrament of Reconciliation.

Individual Rite of Reconciliation

The priest welcomes me in Jesus' name.

I pray the Sign of the Cross.

The priest invites me to trust in God's mercy and love.

I answer:

Help me trace the letters.

AMEN.

The priest may read God's Word in the Bible. Or he may ask me to read it.

I helped color this picture of the Good Shepherd story from the Bible.

I confess my sins. The priest listens. He helps me think about ways to make up for what I did and to do better in the future.

Then the priest gives me a penance. It may be a prayer to pray or a good deed to do.

I tell God I am sorry for my sins.
I pray the Act of Contrition.

My God,
I am sorry for my sins with all my heart.
In choosing to do wrong
and failing to do good,
I have sinned against you
whom I should love above all things.
I firmly intend, with your help,
to do penance,
to sin no more,
and to avoid whatever leads me to sin.
Our Savior Jesus Christ
suffered and died for us.
In his name, my God, have mercy.

If I'd like, I can use my own words to say I'm sorry. This is a prayer I might pray.

Dear God,
I am sorry _____

_____

_____.

Help me _____

_____

_____.

Amen.

The priest prays the words of absolution.

God, the Father of mercies,
through the death and resurrection of his Son
has reconciled the world to himself
and sent the Holy Spirit among us
for the forgiveness of sins;
through the ministry of the Church
may God give you pardon and peace,
and I absolve you from your sins
in the name of the Father, and of the Son,
and of the Holy Spirit.

I answer:

AMEN.

My sins are forgiven. I am reconciled with God and with the Church.

The priest invites me to give thanks to God. He then says "Go in peace" or other words like that. I answer:

Amen.

I might also say:

Thank you, Father.

I leave and do my penance as soon as possible.

Draw a picture of yourself praying.

Here I am praying in thanks to God.
He always loves me.

Communal Rite of Reconciliation

Opening Song

I gather with the parish community. I join with the priest and all those gathered in singing a hymn.

Opening Prayer

The priest greets us and invites all to pray.

We respond:

Amen.

Draw yourself and your family here.

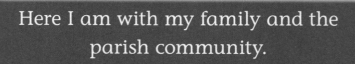

Here I am with my family and the parish community.

Celebration of the Word of God

I listen carefully to the readings from Scripture. Then I listen to the homily. The homily helps me understand God's Word better.

Examination of Conscience

I join the community in an examination of conscience. The priest or deacon may help us by asking questions. We think about how we have or have not been good followers of Jesus.

General Confession of Sin

Then all pray this or another prayer.

I confess to almighty God
and to you, my brothers and sisters,
that I have greatly sinned,
in my thoughts and in my words,
in what I have done and in what I have failed to do,
   [And, striking their breast, they say:]
through my fault, through my fault,
through my most grievous fault;
therefore I ask blessed Mary ever-Virgin,
all the Angels and Saints,
and you, my brothers and sisters,
to pray for me to the Lord our God.

Next the priest or deacon leads us in asking for God's mercy and forgiveness. I answer with everyone:

We pray you, hear us.

Or I might answer:

Lord, have mercy.

Then we all pray the Lord's Prayer aloud.

Individual Confession and Absolution

I wait for my turn to talk with a priest. Then I confess my sins in private.

The priest listens. He helps me think about ways to show my love for God. Then he gives me a penance.

The priest forgives my sins in God's name with the words of absolution. As the prayer ends, I say:

AMEN.

Proclamation of Praise
for God's Mercy

I return to my place and pray quietly.
I praise God for his gift of forgiveness.

Concluding Prayer of Thanksgiving

Then the individual confessions are over.
We sing or say a prayer together to give
thanks to God.

Concluding Rite

The priest blesses us. To each blessing, I answer with everyone:

Amen.

Then the priest or deacon tells us to go in peace. We respond by saying:

Thanks be to God.

God's Love Is Forever

I can celebrate the Sacrament of Reconciliation again when I sin.

I can celebrate God's gift of forgiveness any time and as many times as I want.

I can celebrate the Sacrament of Reconciliation over and over again.

It's your turn to color me.